WORLD MYTHOLOGY

CYCLOPES

B. A. Hoena

Consultant:

Dr. Laurel Bowman
Department of Greek and Roman Studies
University of Victoria
Victoria, British Columbia

Capstone
press

Mankato, Minnesota

Capstone Press
151 Good Counsel Drive, P.O. Box 669, Mankato, Minnesota 56002
http://www.capstonepress.com

Library of Congress Cataloging-in-Publication Data
Hoena, B. A.
    Cyclopes / by B. A. Hoena.
    p. cm. — (World mythology)
    Summary: An introduction to the cyclops characters and their roles in Greek and
Roman mythology.
    ISBN 0-7368-2497-9 (hardcover)
    ISBN 13: 978-0-7368-9634-4 (softcover pbk.)
    ISBN 10: 0-7368-9634-1 (softcover pbk.)
    1. Cyclopes (Greek mythology)—Juvenile literature. [1. Cyclopes (Greek mythology)
2. Mythology, Classical.] I. Title. II. Series: World mythology (Mankato, Minn.)
BL820.C83H64 2004
398.2'0938'01—dc22   2003012974

Editorial Credits
Juliette Peters, series designer; Patrick Dentinger, book designer and illustrator;
    Alta Schaffer, photo researcher; Eric Kudalis, product planning editor

Photo Credits
Art Resource/Réunion des Musées Nationaux, cover; Scala, 8, 10, 18
Bridgeman Art Library/Musee des Beaux-Arts, Rouen, France/Peter Willi, 4;
    Hermitage, St. Petersburg, Russia, 12; Palazzo del Te, Mantua, Italy, 14;
    Villa Romana del Casale, Piazza Armerina, Sicily, Italy, 16
Corbis/Gian Berto Vanni, 20

1 2 3 4 5 6 09 08 07 06 05 04

TABLE OF CONTENTS

Polyphemus throws a rock at Odysseus' ship in Alexandre-Gabriel Decamps' painting *Polyphemus Attacking Sailors in Their Boat*.

CYCLOPES

Ancient Greeks and Romans told stories about one-eyed giants called Cyclopes (sye-KLOH-peez). In some stories, Cyclopes made lightning bolts for the Greek god Zeus (ZOOS). In other stories, Cyclopes threw large rocks at ships and attacked sailors.

People told about the Cyclopes in myths. These stories said the Cyclopes were extremely ugly. Even the gods did not like to look at them. The Cyclopes stood as tall as mountains and were very strong. They also had mean tempers. In one myth, a Cyclops (SYE-klahpss) dropped part of a mountain on a man who made him angry.

Polyphemus (pahl-i-FEE-muhss) is the most well-known Cyclops. He trapped the Greek hero Odysseus (oh-DISS-ee-uhss) in a cave. Polyphemus ate several of Odysseus' companions before the hero found a way to escape.

GREEK and ROMAN *Mythical Figures*

Greek Name: **APOLLO**
Roman Name: **APOLLO**
Zeus' son and god of youth, music, and healing

Greek Name: **ASCLEPIUS**
Roman Name: **AESCULAPIUS**
Apollo's son and god of medicine

Greek Name: **CRONUS**
Roman Name: **SATURN**
Titan who ruled the gods and the sky before Zeus

Greek Name: **GAEA**
Roman Name: **GAEA**
Mother of the first three Cyclopes and goddess of the earth

Greek Name: **GALATEA**
Roman Name: **GALATEA**
Nymph whom Polyphemus loved

Greek Name: **ODYSSEUS**
Roman Name: **ULYSSES**
Hero who blinded Polyphemus

Greek Name: **POLYPHEMUS**
Roman Name: **POLYPHEMUS**
Poseidon's son and one of the Cyclopes

Greek Name: **POSEIDON**
Roman Name: **NEPTUNE**
Zeus' brother, god of the sea, and Polyphemus' father

Greek Name: **URANUS**
Roman Name: **URANUS**
Father of the first three Cyclopes and first god of the sky

Greek Name: **ZEUS**
Roman Name: **JUPITER**
Ruler of the gods

Long ago, people used myths to explain natural events that they did not understand. Ancient Greeks and Romans did not know what caused thunder and lightning. So, people told stories to explain their cause. Myths said the Cyclopes helped create thunder and lightning.

The first three Cyclopes were children of Gaea (GAY-uh) and Uranus (YUR-uh-nuhss). Gaea was the goddess of the earth. Uranus was the first god of the sky.

The three Cyclopes were skilled builders and blacksmiths. They made a magic weapon called a **thunderbolt** for Zeus. The Cyclopes also made lightning bolts. Zeus used the thunderbolt to throw lightning bolts at his enemies.

Ancient Greeks and Romans believed Zeus caused thunder and lightning. The sound of thunder happened when Zeus used his thunderbolt. Lightning was one of Zeus' lightning bolts streaking across the sky.

Benvenuto Cellini's statue *Jupiter* shows the ruler of the gods. Jupiter is the Roman name for Zeus. In his right hand, Jupiter holds the magic thunderbolt that the Cyclopes made for him.

Gaea and Uranus had 12 children called **Titans**. These giants were gods of nature. The Titans controlled the winds and the seas. The Titan Cronus (KROH-nuhss) ruled the sky and the gods.

Cronus was not a kind ruler. He trapped the Cyclopes under the earth. He also imprisoned his own children. Cronus worried that they might grow stronger than he was and **overthrow** him.

Cronus' youngest child, Zeus, got away. Zeus then helped his sisters and brothers escape. Zeus and his **siblings** fled to Mount Olympus in Greece and became known as the **Olympians**.

Zeus knew Cronus might imprison the Olympians again. So, he decided to overthrow Cronus and the other Titans. Zeus freed the Cyclopes and asked them to help overthrow Cronus.

The Cyclopes helped by making magic weapons for the Olympians. For Zeus, they made the thunderbolt. With their magic weapons, the Olympians defeated Cronus. Then, Zeus became ruler of the sky and the gods.

Apollo (right) stands next to the Centaur Chiron (center) in this ancient Roman painting. Chiron taught Asclepius (left) how to heal people.

Apollo was the god of light, music, and healing. He had a human son named Asclepius (ahs-KLEE-pee-uhss). Asclepius was a skilled **healer** like his father.

Myths say Asclepius knew how to bring the dead back to life. Zeus did not want a human to have this power. He killed Asclepius with a lightning bolt.

Apollo was angry at Zeus, but he knew he was not strong enough to harm Zeus. So, Apollo killed the three Cyclopes. They had made the lightning bolt Zeus used to kill Apollo's son.

Zeus punished Apollo for killing the Cyclopes. He made Apollo take care of King Admetus' (ad-MEE-tuhss) cattle for one year. This task embarrassed Apollo.

Later, Zeus felt sorry that he had killed Asclepius. Asclepius had performed many good deeds by healing people who were sick. Zeus brought Asclepius back to life and made him a god of healing and medicine.

Nicolas Poussin's painting *Landscape with Polyphemus* shows the Cyclops Polyphemus (top center) sitting on a mountain. He is playing a love song for Galatea (bottom center, seated on rock).

POLYPHEMUS

Myths tell about another group of Cyclopes. They lived in mountain caves on Sicily. Sicily is an island near Italy.

Some myths say the Cyclopes on Sicily were related to the first three Cyclopes. But they were not as skilled as the first three Cyclopes. The island Cyclopes were neither blacksmiths nor builders. Instead, they raised sheep and goats.

The Cyclops Polyphemus was the son of the sea god Poseidon (poh-SYE-duhn). Polyphemus was the biggest and strongest of the island Cyclopes. Myths say that he liked to sink ships and eat sailors.

One day, Telemus (TE-li-muhss) visited Sicily. Telemus was a **seer** and told people about their future. He told Polyphemus that a great hero would come to Sicily and blind him. At the time, Polyphemus did not listen to Telemus' warning. All Polyphemus thought about was a beautiful sea **nymph** named Galatea (gah-luh-TEE-uh).

Giulio Romano's painting *Polyphemus, Acis, and Galatea* shows
Acis and Galatea (bottom right) hiding from Polyphemus.

Polyphemus loved Galatea, but he worried that she thought he was an ugly monster. So, he combed his messy hair and trimmed his shaggy beard. Polyphemus even sang a love song to impress Galatea.

Galatea did not love Polyphemus. She loved a young man named Acis (UH-siss). Acis was the son of a sea nymph. As Polyphemus sang, Galatea and Acis hid together behind a rock.

After Polyphemus' song was over, Galatea and Acis thought it was safe to come out from their hiding place. But Polyphemus saw them together. He became very angry.

Galatea and Acis tried to flee from Polyphemus. Galatea dived into the ocean, but Acis did not escape. Polyphemus picked up a piece of a mountain and dropped it on Acis.

Acis' blood flowed from under the mountain. Myths say his blood slowly turned to water. Acis' blood became a river that flows from the foot of Mount Etna in Sicily.

This ancient Roman painting shows Odysseus (left) with the Cyclops Polyphemus (right).

POLYPHEMUS AND ODYSSEUS

The Greek hero Odysseus stopped on Sicily as he sailed home after a great war. He went ashore with several of his men. They needed food and fresh water.

Odysseus and his men found a large cave filled with baskets of fruits, vegetables, and cheese. They waited in the cave for the owner of the food to return.

The food belonged to Polyphemus. He led a flock of sheep into the cave. Then, Polyphemus rolled a large rock in front of the cave's entrance. Odysseus and his men were trapped inside.

Odysseus asked Polyphemus if he and his men could have some of the food. Polyphemus laughed. He grabbed two of Odysseus' men, ate them, and then went to sleep.

Odysseus knew he could not kill Polyphemus while the monster slept. Odysseus and his men would be trapped. They could not move the large rock that blocked the cave's entrance. Odysseus needed to think of a plan to escape.

Odysseus and his men are shown blinding Polyphemus on this
Greek vase. Ancient Greeks decorated everyday items like vases,
cups, and bowls with scenes from myths.

ODYSSEUS ESCAPES

In the morning, Polyphemus ate two of Odysseus' men and then led his sheep outside. Polyphemus blocked the cave's entrance with the rock while he was gone. At night, Polyphemus came back and ate two more men before going to sleep.

Odysseus and his men had sharpened a large log while Polyphemus was outside. As Polyphemus slept, they poked the Cyclops in the eye with the log. Polyphemus woke and roared in pain, but he could not see the men to catch them.

In the morning, Polyphemus moved the rock to let his sheep out. He could not see Odysseus and his men. So, Polyphemus stood in the cave's entrance to keep them from escaping. But the men tricked Polyphemus. They tied themselves to the sheep's bellies. The men escaped as the sheep walked out of the cave.

Polyphemus asked his father, Poseidon, to punish Odysseus. For 10 years, Poseidon stopped Odysseus from sailing home. Poseidon raised storms that sunk Odysseus' ships.

The Cyclopean walls around the ancient city of Mycenae, Greece, were built about 3,000 years ago. The city entrance pictured above is called the Lion's Gate.

MYTHOLOGY TODAY

Myths help people learn about ancient **cultures**. Historians are not sure why people imagined monsters with one eye. The idea may have come from ancient blacksmiths. Some experts believe blacksmiths wore an eye patch over one eye to protect it while they worked. Like these blacksmiths, Cyclopes used only one eye. Other experts believe that a group of blacksmiths had tattoos of an eye or a circle on their foreheads. Cyclopes had one eye on their foreheads similar to the blacksmiths' tattoos.

Names from ancient myths are common today. Myths say the Cyclopes made walls by stacking large rocks on top of each other. Today, walls made of large rocks are called Cyclopean walls. In Marvel Enterprises' X-men comic, Cyclops is the name of a superhero. He shoots a powerful red ray from his eyes.

People no longer believe that Greek and Roman myths are true. These myths are now told for people's enjoyment. They are exciting stories about heroes and their adventures.

Adriatic Sea

•Rome

ITALY

N
W • E
S

•Troy

GREECE

Aegean Sea

ITHACA

Thebes

•Athens

Ionian Sea

Sparta

SICILY

KEY

• City

🏔 Mount Olympus

CRETE

SCALE
Miles
0   100   200

0   100   200
Kilometers

Mediterranean Sea

GLOSSARY

ancient (AYN-shunt)—very old

culture (KUHL-chur)—a people's way of life, ideas, art, customs, and traditions

healer (HEE-lur)—a person who cures other people's illnesses; healers in myths often used potions and herbs to cure people.

nymph (NIMF)—a female spirit or goddess found in a meadow, a forest, a mountain, a sea, or a stream

Olympian (oh-LIM-pee-uhn)—one of 12 powerful gods who ruled the world from Mount Olympus

overthrow (oh-vur-THROH)—to defeat and remove a leader from power

seer (SEE-ur)—a person who can see the future

sibling (SIB-ling)—a brother or a sister

thunderbolt (THUHN-dur-bohlt)—Zeus' magic weapon; Zeus used the thunderbolt to throw lightning bolts at his enemies.

Titan (TYE-ten)—one of 12 giants who ruled the world before the Olympians

READ MORE

Fanelli, Sara. *Mythological Monsters of Ancient Greece.* Cambridge, Mass.: Candlewick Press, 2002.

Hoena, B. A. *Odysseus.* World Mythology. Mankato, Minn.: Capstone Press, 2004.

USEFUL ADDRESSES

National Junior Classical League
422 Wells Mill Drive
Miami University
Oxford, OH 45056

Ontario Classical Association
P.O. Box 19505
55 Bloor Street West
Toronto, ON M4W 1A5
Canada

INTERNET SITES

FactHound offers a safe, fun way to find Internet sites related to this book. All of the sites on FactHound have been researched by our staff.

Here's how:
1. Visit *www.facthound.com*
2. Type in this special code **0736824979** for age-appropriate sites. Or, enter a search word related to this book for a more general search.
3. Click on the **Fetch It** button.

FactHound will fetch the best sites for you!

INDEX